W0259520

TALIBAN
BEACH PARTY

5. Breakfast

This trembling coffee in the cup
is like the ideas inside my forehead:
shifting, uncertain in the wavering light.
I want more light on my thoughts,
I want to discover once and for all
what I can know and not know.
Only then will I be able to grasp
what the eyes see looking inward.

6. Noon

In the daydream I am lost in a field of wheat,
miles of wheat stretching to the horizon.
The stalks rustle higher than my head,
shaking and hissing like a golden fire,
but not a fire, what was once a fire —
dry stalks of flame, as if the field
is the surface of the sun after its death.
Then I am high above the field and see
that it is nothing more than a sunflower
and I strain to find myself crawling alone
among the roots of its blackened seeds.

the people on the streets
are hushed and look up,
refusing to move, knowing
this moment cannot last.

3. Waking

A muffled shout.
and then the white horse
vaulting through the window
and standing steaming
and trembling by the bed,
staring into the sunlight,
stomping, shaking its head.

4. The Return

My hands let go of the sky
and I float down into my body.
My feet and the floorboards
are strangers once again,
but they hold on to one another
like lovers who have been apart
for longer than they can remember.

TALIBAN BEACH PARTY

Eric Howard

TURTLE POINT PRESS
BROOKLYN, NEW YORK

Turtle Point Press
208 Java Street, 5TH Floor
Brooklyn, NY 11222
WWW.TURTLEPOINTPRESS.COM

Book design by Jess Puglisi

Library of Congress Cataloging-in-Publication Data is available from the publisher upon request

ISBN: 978-1-933527-89-5

Printed in the United States of America

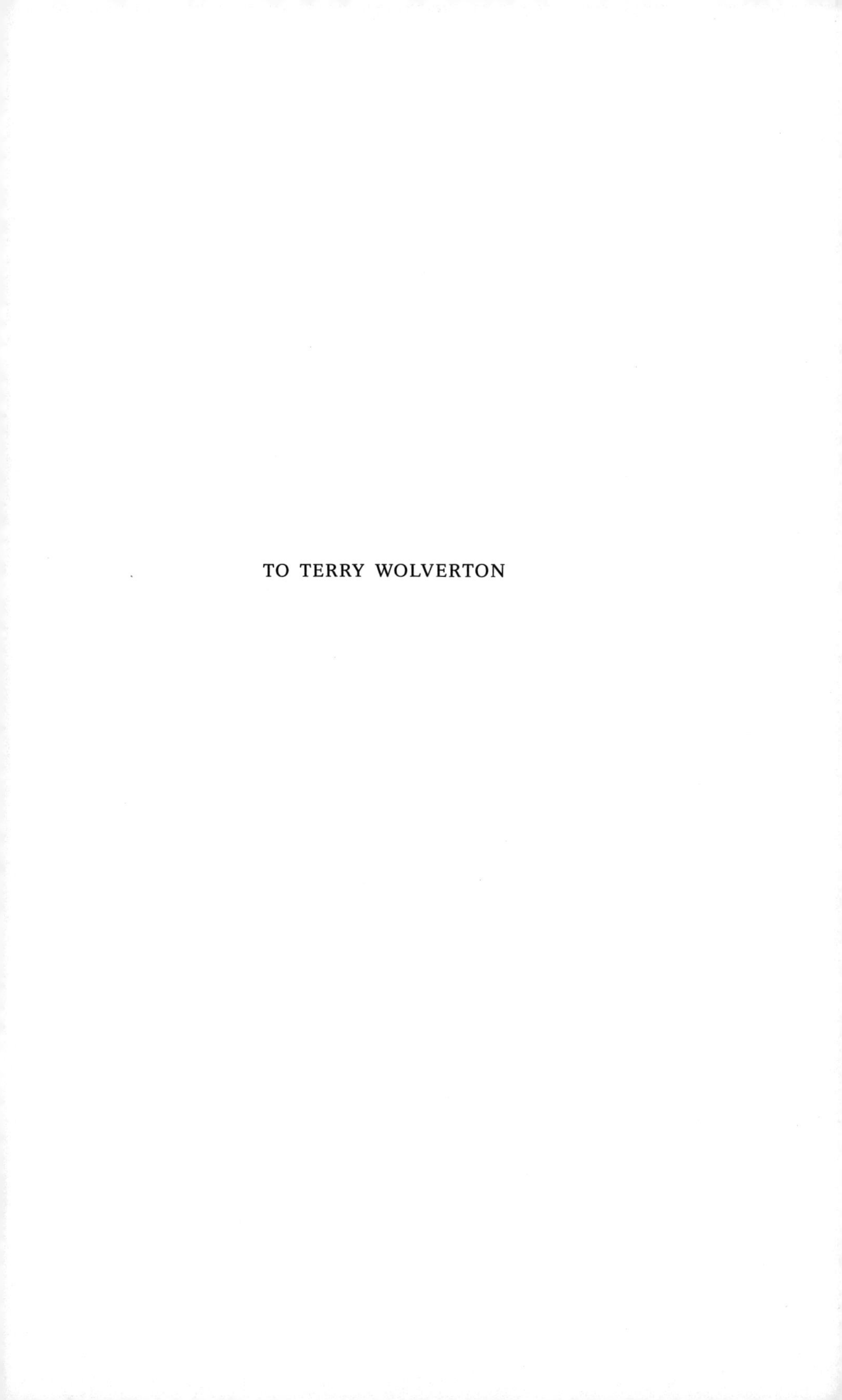

TO TERRY WOLVERTON

Contents

RIDING TO THE L.A. RIVER BIKE PATH

No more, Venus. I am not what I was
when Carol ruled, thanks to you, over me.
I'm pushing 50, in bicycle shorts,
pedaling over the hill past Jula's house.
You'd love her purple hair. She sings and plays
the autoharp, and Brad parks his Harley
in her driveway. Her house has a wood-beamed
ceiling stained by Nag Champa. Bother her.
My cold heart says no more getting blind drunk
at parties at Michael's place. He leaves cute
girls smiling in their sleeping bags after
dancing three days at Burning Man. Would you
leave my bulging prostate and liver alone?
No, you have me ride along the river
where these packs of lean-jawed, tatted Jareds
go racing and I go panting on curves
by poplars and electric towers, wings
of birds rising by ankle and helmet,
your red-faced slave, along the green water.

EL CAMINO

Caminante, no hay camino,
se hace camino al andar.

My neighbor works on his El Camino
under the cottonwood that's pushing up the sidewalk.
He's got the engine rumbling right,
but it needs bodywork and paint.

I roll my bike through the gap in the chain link
by Raul's trailer and start by riding
slow, because kids play in the little green park,
as the homeless guy with prison tats
reminded me with yelled threats of a beatdown
after making me stop by standing spreadeagle across
the path

near where Machado might push his young bride
in her wood wheelchair
by poplar trees like those they knew.

Farther north I can go
faster, hearing the wind for miles
without feet touching ground
where the heron feeds,
to put a mind at peace for a time,
and homeless Whitman loafs
in the empty cactus park.
Over the culvert the crow
glides by, letting things be like this, between
the freeway and the killdeer,
my tires leaving no mark on the concrete,
my shadow no wake in the river.

AT THE TOP OF MOUNT HOLLYWOOD DRIVE

The freeway's out of hearing here. Just wind
in pines where I stop after riding up,
the city in silence below. Hikers
walk by and ask, "Is the Hollywood Sign
that way?" pointing down the road. I say yes,
having learned to lie, because the truth takes
too long to say—the sign is off limits,
well fenced against taggers and suicides,
that it isn't found on Mount Hollywood
but about a mile west, and the road
leads down the wrong slope. Like Kafka's castle,
the sign is only for seeing, not for
getting up close. Too many words for this
quiet place of drought-browned grass waiting to burn.

VAUX SWIFTS

Before they return to the brick chimney
on Broadway—one of the few that remain—
in a living whirlwind to roost for the night
they fly upstream to where the water's wide
and shallow to feed on the flying bugs
so newly alive and driven to mate
that they risk quick death by less than an ounce
of muscle and beak. The sun sets; the bugs
seek branches, and the swifts descend to drink
socially on the concrete riverbed
as I cycle by alone, mercy-free.

TERRITORY

The gate to Mount Hollywood Drive is closed,
but sometimes shiny work trucks will appear.
Electric cables along the roadside,
cherry pickers with spotlights, traffic cones,
and security guards claim half a mile
of fake snow where yesterday coyotes
walked with all the confidence of actors.

A FOOL'S JOURNEY

for Heather Wylie

I'll walk by the L.A. River tonight
above the herons and below the trains
and count the trees bent and draped
in shredded plastic after heavy rains.
I'll give a scallop-shell my confession
and tar my skull
to make a hull
that's wisdomtight.
Let me float past the train yard and station
to where the river drains
past the giant shipping cranes
and let the tide take me to sea.
I'm sorry, said the note she taped
to the fridge, *really*. Verily, verily,
life is but steam. From the cooler I'll pull
my bottle of salvation.
The waves will roll their eyes and sigh.
I'll be a boat of fool.

TO SACKS, A COSTUMER

The dead tell the living
play your part well, for the fashion

of your world is passing.
To be remembered,

remember you have no choice
when she licks the thread

and threads the spool
of your life on her machine.

You want the story to start there
but it's not even the story,

which starts in the rain with a woman
walking down a street in a 40s

raincoat with hidden buttons,
in tears because she's lost

and soaked from scarf to pumps,
who steps in an icy puddle

in front of a good-looking guy,
size 40 trenchcoat, and the fedora

without the bullet hole.
That's where the story starts,

with the studio rain that's from
a river that rose from steam

over seas through goats
and presidents and the dead,

that's immortal like one
who listens to a song

in her head as she keeps
her eye on the blurry needle

and the scene where two fools meet
plays like a movie in her mind,

knowing her silk confections
will be ruined by the water

and every mortal fluid
knotted to each other, even as

her hands flow unseen, sewing a seam.

TALIBAN BEACH PARTY

We threw one at Dockweiler, with costumes
borrowed from studios or sewn in shops.
Three frugging ululating Burkaettes
backed up befezzed, purple tux'd emcee Dan
at the mic as he called the wrestling match.

"In this corner," he bellowed, "weighing two
hundred ninety all-American pounds
and towering tall at five feet and nine
inches, give it up" (cheers) "for Sandra Dee!"
(played by David, the hairy leatherman,
wearing a yellow polka dot bikini,
blond wig, and seaweed wreath, on surfboard laid)

"And in this corner" (boos) "tipping the scales
of injustice at just ninety-nine pounds
and standing six evil feet, O.B.L."
(in camo, fake beard, and turban: Norah,
emo junkie drummer for Waxie Snatch)

Norah raised a Koran above her head
and hollered. David flirtily giggled.

"Place your bets and get ready to rumble!"
Good and Evil fought; Norah bit the sand,
and I (as Jesus) passed out some tuna
sandwiches. I glanced over to Sharon
(as Patty, in trench coat and beret)
who simply pointed me, with her Uzi,
to the fireworks and booze, because jumbo jets
pushing off from LAX swept so low

above our heads that we could see the grime
that streaked their bellies but never be heard.

But Mullah Mixmastah tried with Dick Dale's
reverberating wails turned up to ten
while in celebration of Gidget's win
we barked in tiki and fed our bonfire
pallets and fireworks so the Big Kahuna
would see it burn so high that he would sing
our praises to the planet's satellites.

Diddles the Clown sang naked by the fire
"errybudy's hur tha bir is the whir"
before walking into the dark to give
his Bushmills back to our mother the sea.

As the fire died I sat with marshmallow
beside Clio, who named between takeoffs
gray towns like Budapest and Teplice
that Miki Dora and Frederick Kohner,
upon visions of summer days well spent,
left to build a new kingdom on the coast.
They sin, and I'll sin; they fly, and I'll fly.

To us natives it was naiveté.
What they made was just a fantasy land
to those who grew up here for a "career"
in continuity for Illusion, Inc.
We knew different—thought we knew better,
because the mighty Wurlitzer's last riff
is death in a crappy Hollywood apartment,

with empty bourbon bottles on unpaid
bills around the sink, a hungry yappy
Pekingese scratching the door all damn day.

Clio was boring, so I looked away,
saw a figure veiled in shadow. It could
have been the ghost of Marie Prevost.
But whoever it was did not speak, so
I turned back again to look at embers
in the fire pit, when the boiling amber
in a pine cone burst into a cloud of sparks
that burned as long as any victory cry.

ODE TO ROUTINE

Mr. Sand climbs the back stairs to his desk
and wrinkles his face at the hourglass
that mocks his deadlines in grainy burlesque
of time that spins his pallets of laughing gas
and oxygen away from the right docks.
His frozen computer won't scrape
    the barnacles from clocks
across the region. He cannot escape
the Operations boss coming his way.
Sweaty clouds besiege his balding castle
but can't make boxes walk or dollars pray
to stay where they are. He knew some hassle
like this would come to blast his end-of-year.
To sleep tonight, he'll need more pills and beer.

Dune Woman covers for someone sicker
with more than a hundred orders to fill.
Old fluorescent volts above her flicker
as she pushes tons of paperwork uphill
into the drawer where her head disappears.
The folders of her devotion,
    a library of tears,
will be recycled on March 31,
soon after severance; all her invoices
will feed the big shredder, and all those days
spent making a dozen tiny choices
will pass like parades of traffic in praise
of Routine that drop-shipped her youth, the king
of morning promises and their breaking.

Praise every employee of every week.
The ghost of breath, blood pressure, and heartbeat,
you schedule the stars and hide where we seek
fresh donuts and daydreams and find defeat.
Hooray, *Dental Supplier News* Manager of the Month.
Goodbye, *Dental Supplier News* Manager of the Month.

TRAVELING MAN

Like a cherry stem, a twist was all it took;
trees writhed on the road. The wind took it all.

I fucked up my way when the highway was better,
stuck out thumb and walked; the street took it all.

Walking home after a $300 day—
they say, wassup? Gang took it all.

I sought in Spain a Shangri-la, puked
on a nun in a hotel. Sangría took it all.

I swept until darkness fell, motel
at dawn. My house gone. I took it all.

A palace could have been mine. I sleep
on warehouse pallets. I mistook it all;

I'm to blame; I wanted to start over,
but no revolution's coming. Time took it all.

THE GREAT RUMBLE

Among the drought-dirty
work trucks
we look up to see the 5's
exhaust-black steel beams
on great concrete
pillars—
tense homeowners
unheeded day laborers
and pigeons—
feeling the deep howl
and clang of the wheels
above the big chain
hardware store's
parking lot.

TO THE TERRACE HOUSE

It was good to see your guts knocked out
enough to fill six truck containers
and a new house rise from your frame
after selling your aluminum-sided,
earthquake-crooked fugliness.

I regret kicking everyone out of you—
the drunk punk and lame director,
the wannabe P.A. who slept in your shed,
Drummer Girl, a crackhead, a family,
and, finally, me. Your cracks where
silverfish, ants, and roaches stampeded
have left like the black widow that charged
out between my eyeballs as I wrenched your drain.
No more crawlies with countless knees
that waved like Misfit mohawks
complicate the porn shoot, 500 bucks for your bills,
where I learned the proper rolling of extension cords.

Goodbye, shed that no band played in,
soundproofed too late to get Drummer Girl back.
I am grateful for your coffee pot
and happy pills, work by 8:30, boss says Saturdays too,
three million words by Thanksgiving's greasy duck
I cooked for her just once. I respect
your 70s shag carpet that my demented cat
used as a toilet. Thank you, overflowing toilets,
retaining walls that didn't,
and water heater that puked to death
and curled the floor. Goodbye,
Surrealist bathroom and refrigerator,

and Sor Juana Inés de la Cruz,
the hunchback iguana raised on burritos and Diet Sprite.
For your mortgage I taught
English 96 at the local CC, more
students than chairs the first night.
Bless my evaluator's bourbon breath.
I bid goodbye to the neighbor's spite fence.

Everyone who lived in you—teacher,
mother, faith healer, in-betweener—
picked from the fruit trees of your *bolgia*.
Goodbye, smoking air conditioner,
unplumb doors and untrue floors,
houseplants dying in galvanized buckets,
and 436 thousand fuckits. I miss
Sticky Nikki and Chuckles,
who came to collect from the psycho
Satanist *Playboy* model, Severina,
who after getting high in the bathtub
was as gone as the bullet hole
in your kitchen wall is now. I washed away
the red paint *DIE!* with pentacle
from your broken gate. From the chair
on your porch I contemplated
the snow tire, on a wheel, that bounded
through the glass door and thumped twice,
its studs ripping carpet, before going
through a window and down the hill. A burglar
took a boombox through that window after it was fixed.

Goodbye, bedroom that Drummer Girl
didn't come back to till morning
when I left for work and she cranked "Ænema."

Ave atque vale, Halloween party I threw
to let her go with, waking up alone on the couch,
door open, various vomits. So long, 300-yard
restraining order circling you and me both.
I'll let go of the 100 drunk attempts to have
that sex again with someone else. Bless
the notches in the shotgun choke
I pressed above my Adam's apple,
brain out of reasons. After a shiver, one—
I'd cause more pain. She said I loved you more than her.

She was love. You were duty. I failed both
and the picture of her in my sweatshirt,
drumming, in the album with mostly empty pages,
by setting it on fire and watching it turn black,
curl cancerous smoke below your grapefruit.
I'll let fall those 50-pound bags of gravel
I shouldered down every step to the last level,
when the sun flexed like a drum, like a heart attack.

DRUMMER GIRL'S KANJI BOOKS

You worked for the yakuza
  then the lawyers at Disney

Live Sex Show!
  answer the phones

your first set of drums left to a Tenderloin punk house
  file the papers

learned Japanese, spiked speed
  your bosses made

forged diplomas for art school
  with such schooling.

Remembering the Kanji:
A complete course on how not to forget
the meaning of characters

Using imaginative memory

The salarymen put tokens in the machine
  looking through your office window

to stare at you, just turned adult, thin and small
  fantasizing songs

The Filipinas didn't want to like you, dyed blonde American,
  powerless

but you they helped
  over the beat of wake work sleep.

  You left the books on my shelf when I told you to leave.
    Shelf, a book's good companion

Did you know those years ago you'd ask

    Think of reading turtle-backs
    as a way to foretell the future—

  to spend a couple hours
  fucking to feel holy
  on a rough stained besdspread
  in a dirty Googie motel,
  Cramps on the boom box
  by the box of chicken,
  its smell braiding with your cigarette smoke,
  and my knife holding Gideon's
  open on Revelation 17?

    Live(ly), tongues babbling like water
    Sex, plants and the earth from which they spring
    Show, altar

  to try to bring you back I only have to open any page:

    Love, birdhouse . . . walking.

WALKING ALONG SUNSET WEIGHING PIECES OF PLASTIC WITH MY DRUG DEALER'S POCKET SCALE

In the shadow of the air raid siren
on Parkman
eyes go to the gutter
that goes to the Pacific

    forks, two, white
all life is breath on a ball
    small grocery bag
    broken clothing tag tie, red,

thread-thin, less
than a centigram, with a cross
at one end to catch inside
some finger-size fish

the great garbage patch
coughs up tons on Laysan
    bar code tag, white,
    DVD box latch, black,

    eyeglass temple, tortoiseshell
where maybe now some grad student
weighs dead birds twice
    bar code sticker, white

once with plastic
and once without,
twenty-four grams per chick
    RFID chip housing, .52g,

When she comes back home,
She'll be the weirdo at the wedding
10-amp car fuse housing, red, .2g,
talking of albatross and parts per million

and the Permian, filaments
of nylon, beaks and bones
flowery glistening polypropylene
borne on the birthplace of Venus

lighter, translucent blue

HOLLYWOOD RIDE

We sped through gaps
between the steel cattle,
around the bending bus
of tired workers, by
thumping Hummers, cheap
ricers, Eurobling, jacked-up trucks,
wastes of neckbeard fat on chromed
unmuffled Harleys, and one
party bus, music and blue lights
behind glass, war breath
of tailpipes on our calves
that rolled faster on the boulevard's
crushed glass and asphalt glam than all
the horsepower stuck
in each other's parade, and
the bravest of us mashed it
through reds at the front
of the pack, a Marlboro
angled on what-of-it lips,
another Robert Mitchum at 20
on a black fixie with suicide bars,
dodging potholes and cars
as we wheeled past cult HQs,
fake superheroes walking on stars
and concrete autographs, a pack
of homeless kids giving us shouts
outside the crowded mall, but
security said get out, so we ran
circles in the parking lot,
turned back home.

Then from behind
the vato peloton she shot
forward helmetless with no lights,
her long black hair like two handfuls
of money let loose into the wind.

DIESEL

Here between the river
and the freeway

a quarter million cars per day
rhyme oxygen and fuel

fine enough to lodge
in lungs or cross

the blood-brain barrier
of all the people in the circle

of my hearing
breathing tire

dust and Jake brake coughs
feeling the train engines

shake the sky, the car
thumping corridos,

geese honking
as they climb the grainy sky.

APOSTROPHE

Why shouldn't I love you?
You're a spit curl,

a hat that cants
where you stand

without a wearer. Or
you're a raised

club of absence
or possession, a

mixed message like
a pope's Torah.

Sibilant speck, don't be
apropos, play those p's and q's.

Help me earn
by bein' hard to learn.

TO PTSD

I scare a kid by sitting at her table,
and I hear you when I think at her
get out, you high school cafeteria geek.
She leaves because I look like
some old weirdo-beware-movie freak
who just wants coffee now, just like
I wanted coffee then, and to be alone,
when a different kid, some high school geek,
waited a week of mornings outside my door
when I was a teacher before he curled
his knuckle and made his blood knock. Your friends,
those green and yellow pills, wiped years
of yellow topic sentences off the green board
and turned the yearbooks gray, but failed
to unbang his gun or roll his eyes down,
so I can only praise you, surly boy brushing
backpack past me now, you impossible
high school geek, as my hands cup my coffee
in a concentric shudder, praise how you taught me
why I must and why I can't
stand on this table and tell them all
I love you, you beautiful high school geeks.

SIDE EFFECTS MAY INCLUDE

Amanuensis of the hand on the sides of your life
Bipedalism across the young plains in a fur bikini
Curtilage of the tongue and throat
Demurrage for the weight of the smoke
Easement for symptoms that may persist because
  you're alive
Fraud upon your house
Gog and Magog across the San Fernando Valley
Hermeneutics of fire giants running uphill
Imminence of horror and latex
Joinder to *Yellow Wallpaper v. Gregor the Beetle*
Kenosis of the bath house and porn set
Laches of "you know I still love you"
Mitosis of some happy dayglow chick
Noema of the man from nowhere on trial for murder
Orderliness of the refrigerators that will be cleaned
  out at 3 P.M.
Periphrasis for diving into meat grinders
Quintillions of first years of service
Replevin of the Worldwide Mad Deadly Hollywood
  Gangster Computer God
Spam from ghosts of your past lives
Transubstantiation of all the numbers of the phone
  system
Unclean hands upon the world
Viscosity of ketchup or Tapatío
Warbling of pharmacists at Kaiser on Sunset
Xylographia five years experience $10 an hour
Yodeling internship opportunity
Zarzuela of stars and hangers-on and homeless

WHAT MOSES LOOKED LIKE

Dan was a Jewish-Italian hoodlum
with scarred hands and a junkie's white T-shirt.
Moira had porcelain skin and red hair
with white streaks that flowed from both temples.
Moses, like Grandpa Munster—
sometimes people asked him for autographs.
He'd tell stories about the show as he signed.

After surgeons raided Daddy Mo's thighs
for a quadruple bypass, he told me
"It isn't all about you" when I asked
why he hadn't called. He only let Dan
help pull his "pantyhose" on (not his thing),
and stopped calling me for rides, complaining,
"Why you gotta drive so meshugganah?"

Before he died, he'd cruise his Cadillac
Cimarron out to Santa Monica
to watch the sun set into the ocean
between him and a promised land of bars
with go-go boys and cash in his pocket.

He liked being free when California
let his person go to a halfway house
with a bare wood floor down by Alvarado
and Third, near where a dealer's hollow point
chewed up Dan's shoulder and swallowed Mo's house
just off Selma with the porch filled with failed
Shakespeare company props: fake swords and chairs
of stained pine and red velvet where Moira
the alcoholic driver and the day's boys
drank until the hills called an audition.

Mo would draw my naked feet while Dan yelled
"You're a rat bastard" at *The People's Court*.
What we loved the most was *Henry IV*.
"Falstaff sweats to death," Dan would mock fat Mo,
"and lards the lean earth as he walks along."
We laughed at Daddy Mo. We pitied him.

MOIRA AT THE DOOR

You could say she reigned
behind a thrift store student desk
her *Bride of Frankenstein* hair

at the head of the line that wound
into the alley
below the neon sign for the

taxi dance place upstairs.
The white box gallery
near Spring and 9th

shut the front door and opened the back
Fridays and Saturdays for men,
women on Sundays.

That she bestowed the hand stamp,
was the fiduciary of the gray
metal cash box. She read

a true crime paperback
once the sex party started
not much to do

but wait for sunrise and cleanup.

HOW A FLOWER BECAME A STONE

Transparent Mercury flew just above
a car-crushed Los Angeles boulevard,
his wings strumming the power lines around
a college field, startling the pigeons flocked
for postgame popcorn into flight. He looped
the floodlights bugs spun in, saw Rocío
lead her soccer team to another goal,
and rose and spread his wings wide to slow down
and let his eyes expand at her ponytailed
shapeliness and quick footwork that outshone
the other adolescents on the grass.

A New Year's Eve bullet that's fired skyward,
however leaden and dull, can briefly
soar and glow with heat and danger; likewise
the god of speed and cunning spiraled down
to allow his feet to touch ground and stop
thinking. He took his real form, all movie
star handsome, but still smoothed his sun-bleached hair
and purple tracksuit and practiced a smile.
His Nikes glowing white, he caught her eye
just once as she ran, then turned and faded
into the crowd and air. She forgot him.

Instantly he knocked on her house's door
and when her mother, Flora, answered, she
turned the TV off and smiled, believing
nothing of his story, really, but charmed
by the supposed talent scout. She took
his business card and nodded a promise.

Chaste Athena watched it all on her phone
and did not approve of what Mercury
had in mind. From her olive tree-shrouded
Mount Olympus midcentury she flew down
to the cheap sullen flats of East Hollywood,
where she knew a grungy frizzy-haired drunk
named Ivy, whose dark cluttered apartment
belched the smell of cats and old wet cat food
when she opened the door and muttered some
unpleasantries about how her cousin
only came when she needed a favor.
But deals with poor relatives come easy,
and Ivy soon flew off with Athena
to visit Rocío's mom. The survey
trick worked: a clipboard and a free sample
that Ivy gave Flora with poisoned touch
of hand to hand. Before closing the door
to the second stranger that day—which was odd,
Flora thought—she began to brood. The sun
set. Her mood darkened. She flipped through channels
and raided the fridge, but nothing pleased her.
Was she so old, so poor, and so shabby
she had to help some sleazeball meet her daughter?

Her brow wilted and tongue turned sour as she
waited for Rocío to get home. And
right after she did, Mercury returned,
an assortment of costly inducements
distributed in his tracksuit's pockets,
But still she refused to let him inside. He begged,
flattered, and reminded her of their deal,
but still she refused to unlock the door.

Mercury's short fuse ran out. Before she
could even think to stop she raised one arm
to flip him off, and felt her next impulse—
which was to close the door—go nowhere.
Her last "fuck off, creep" failed to reach her mouth
from her hardening brain; she couldn't move
her eyes to see he had turned her to stone
for having broken a promise to a god.

THE FATES ON LOCATION

Something bad is going to come of this. RICHARD NIXON

They were tired of crowding into taxis that smelled of
cigarettes and so many transitory lives reminding
them that they were legally blind and could not drive
in Los Angeles, tired of wearing the same clothes at
2 A.M. that they'd put on day before,

tired of filling out expense reports for the shadows
surrounding those photographs of the senator on the
concrete floor, grimacing with his legs splayed,

of being kept awake by crickets even in third-floor hotel
rooms in the middle of the city,

of ensuring that William Barry tell him, "No, it's been
changed, we're going this way,"

of hanging heavy crosses on the shoulders of seventeen-
year-old busboys who happened to be shaking
Bobby's hand the moment before,

of tending to all the details like steering the crazy
shooter who'd gotten drunk toward the hotel coffee
urn rather than the back seat of his car to sleep it off,

of rosaries pressed into dying hands, of suit coats put
into use as pillows, of guiding bullets with awful
grace into five bystanders exactly as required,

of hearing Bobby ask “Is everybody OK?” his blood
slowly pooling on the passageway floor between the
steam table and the ice machine,

of the war ending him rather than him ending the war,

of cameras that can’t run backward, and the reporter
asking “Is it possible?” into his reel-to-reel tape
recorder,

of the silence of the young campaigner in her straw hat
holding her face in her hands,

of how weak they felt knowing all the rolls to develop,
frames to count, and final cuts to be made,

how they’d have to fly across the country to guide
his funeral procession through a shantytown called
Resurrection City,

how they were getting older all the time while the job
kept getting harder, and they had to get in the taxi
and keep going, day following day with death their
unobtainable goal.

REDHEAD VENUS

She was the suicide vest
he strapped to his chest that made
his eyeballs fly across the market.

She read him *Comus* in bed
then turned the boombox up
so Dylan could sing his sorrows
and lamentations so loud
that the bum in the alley
rolling an empty 40 under his palm
couldn't hear them.

The smell from the bakery filled the room.
Now at the market he buys challah
and puts the bag to his face like a huffer
but it doesn't bring back her closet
where he smelled her clothes, a disloyal dog,
for three winters and four summers.

She read, "Being smeared with grease,
brimstone, and gunpowder, they cried,
'Salt on, salt on this sinful and rotten flesh!'
Their tongues were cut out,
and they were afterward committed to the flames,
which soon consumed them,"
while he made potatoes au gratin.
They licked their plates in the old kitchen
painted so many times the drawers were sticky.

The body aflame
He pressed her against the stove, and she told him
when he made her come she felt
like a gangster staggered by machine gun fire.

the mind aflame
Past the shimmering magazine rack,
into the alley off Fairfax,
he'd call up for her to let him in
and share fresh challah from the bakery
across the alley, allies for a time.

experienced as pleasure
The fire, making the appearance of a vault,
like the sail of a vessel filled by the wind,
made a wall around the body of the martyr
not like flesh burning, but like a loaf in the oven.

with aging and death disenchanted
He said he was sorry, but nothing fixed it,
not the time he got up before sunrise
to watch her surfing in her wetsuit
by the pier when he wanted coffee,
his brain burning and shoes filling up with sand.

with distresses and despairs
What was wrong with him
that he could ever not want her
redheadedly wanting him?

Now he sees the women at the market but remembers her.

NOT OK CUPID

You sit in the back of class because you already
  know everything,
  dumb as a peacock's tail.
You love on condition of darkness
  believing in the justice of desire,
  hot brand fryin' eyeball.
Elvis gold suit Can't Be Wrong.
You get drunk phone calls at 3 A.M., start fights you
  don't finish.
Cupid you play guitar and sing boleros to a roomful
  of lovers and go back to your motel alone.
Cupid you don't have an explanation for last night.
Cupid she lies beside her fat drunk sweaty snoring
  husband and remembers you.
Cupid, fuck and run, change your name and lie.
Cupid dead at 24 of a heroin overdose to the surprise of
  no one.
Cupid you swallowed arsenic in a garret and drowned
  one summer day in a storm,
  a book of Keats in your pocket.
Cupid the surfer god all through high school
  and six years of college,
  pills and vodka in your van by the beach.

You weren't invited to the picnic but showed up anyway.
With curly hair and dimples you rocked "Satisfaction"
  at karaoke and went home to watch *Love Boat* reruns
  in your underwear.

Cupid sitting zen can't stop thinking about that time
  with Jenny in the 12th grade.
Cupid you make her wish she could turn the car around.

Cupid you are the tyrant's nightmare
  with your pompadour and black leather jacket,
  you ride a Harley that pushes harder than death.
The mobster checking his watch in the club
  never knew you assfucked
  his 20-year-old model
  girlfriend in the back seat of the limo.
Cupid in church you see her black hair two rows up
  and try to catch her eye with your Serious Face.
Cupid come back,
  easy to kiss at night,
  hard to let go come morning
  until she got the abortion while you went surfing.
Cupid you never learn don't ever change.
Like a mountain wind bending the oaks
  you run through the forest at night
  as a husband fires his shotgun at where you were.
You shower in the morning while she sings and
  makes eggs.
You make promises like a teenage girl does to Jesus.

TO FORTUNA

Let us now praise Random Chance
the heavens wheeling cloudy
spokes that wobble like
roulette wheels on gambling boats

Quantum and celestial
mechanics hear her noises
in the curvature of ants
along a growing vine

fuzzing up the sign
in numbers that rain
katamari proteins
and migratory stars

from drops and strands
the Goddess of Whatever
has a holy family made
About her throne of falling feathers

darts arc where angels dirty dance
She alone is as tolerant
as empty space and funny looking
only to those who will not see

her flowers in the fly's ad hoc
buzzings and how they fly
through all creation just sticks and string
plucked to the beat of that RC swing

MARK

I believe you believe.
She believes we open
and sort attachments, spam
and resumes. They say
we're making an impression.
My eyes dart after the ball
among the dancing cups.
You believe your finger
is on the button but
the TV is still on.
It's unbelievable
that seeing they may see.
Has she elegance? Has she fragrance?
They say the con man's son
has hanged himself in shame,
didn't know the business
he was in. We never
see the x's on our backs.
You finger every stack
of green prayers changing from
my hands to hers to theirs.
In God we trust. I believe
in you, and you me.

THE EMPRESS

I mother chrysalis and cell and hide
my voice in fortune teller gibberish
I wove into acid that sings when I knead
new silver fish to warm penguin bellies.
I hear silkworms chewing mulberry leaves
and teach the garden wasps to roll to me
the pomegranates that I like to eat
while my kittens sleep in sunlight. I seed
the forests, color cuttlefish and beetles.

In my womb breathe the seeds of all monsters.
Disobey my moons, and time may come they
shrivel you. Rob me, and I'll come for you.
Blanketed in bats, I'll cross Hell barefoot
to trouble your door. Open it, or I
will smash its frame and take back what you stole,
grind your bones for my tomatoes, and forget
your name. Come, ask your question, child.
Some tea? Talk to me. I know your mother.

THE DEATH OF MY GREAT-GRANDMOTHER

One minute out on Route 78 south,
in a big four-door with a radio, she rolled
her window down, let her hand
cup and carve the desert air
that fluttered her collar bow, and smiled.

Above the sand, the cornea
of sky arched. Cousin Larry
was driving, friends Beth and Teddy Rupp
in back. Her baby was safe at home,
two weeks' pay in her purse. What
she wanted was a Coke on ice in Felicity.

The radio played a song to hum to.
Then she pushed knuckles to her cheeks and
  stuck out her tongue,
just for a laugh. Beth, the one about to live,
smiled and said, "Mae, you cuttin' up."

WHITE TRASH MOUSE

My mother, born in the Depression,
wanted a two-car heaven
and gave me a name middle-class enough
to shake all the Alabama drunks
from her hairbrush. It kinda
worked. Even after half
a century in libraries, I know there's no point
to reading up on the Norseman
who splashed his face with his enemies' blood,
but like them kin
I think no problem can't be solved
with Vice Grips and a 3/8-inch drill.
Unlike them, I learned the maze
well enough to sneak
thru the mirror
into wine-and-cheese parties,
and other people's papers
to rent a garage in Silver Lake
and go foraging in bars
incontinent with disco
feeling and smelling in the dark
to the beer-and-a-grope
cinderblock wall that blooms with jasmine.
Before dumping me, my doe
spent weeks clicking herself
back to Germany on Ancestry.com.
She told me I should look myself up,
but I never did, because why the hell
would I want to know which poorhouse
my DNA dragged itself out of?

BLIND DATE

"What does this lesbian want, Cupid?"
I asked when I saw her. "To please her father, stupid."

THE UNICORN

When fire sweeps the grass, horses flee with me,
but they unherd me back to pink bedrooms
to fart rainbows and shake glitter from my mane.
If I lived, I'd care. In Shakespeare's sonnets
some refuse to see me, and most who don't
express concern about my poison blood.
Curio described Caesar so: every
woman's man and every man's woman,
natural and unnatural, like Pegasus.
I broke my horn against a wall but grew
a new one back. Sex fiction Carrie Bradshaw
denied me after riding me, but I can't
blame her. Sometimes even I can't decide
and close my eyes and dream about leaving
this so-called forest for the rough pine planks
of a mirror-balled barn I can hide in.

BOY OR GIRL

Scant years before that my sixteenth year I still lived with my parents and grew my hair long, Angel Bowie had come down from his spaceship and blessed my kind before the world, so being a kid I was surprised to hear that harsh breath behind me as a football player, running full speed, tackled me from behind, still surprised as I got up on all fours and he grabbed me there hard and yelled at his friends, "It's a boy!" and they laughed, leaning on the pedestal of the marble St. Augustine that stood on with his staff at the entrance to the school I was about to get expelled from for being blasphemy.

PSYCHOLOGY TODAY

Going home from my girlfriend's after
she said she loved me but didn't want to live together,
I stopped at the newsstand. There was this story
of a woman who had slept as a man and woman
with men and women that made me
stop wondering if the guy by the car magazines
would pick me up. Was she real?
Or was she just made up to fill
a page's deadline as sharp
as the this-ain't-the-library look
the old newsstand guy gave me through two
curved mirrors when I chanced to look up?

VENUS XTRAVAGANZA

Behold her
at the Christopher Street Pier,
Big blonde hair by red and black graffiti,
sunset over the dirty
little black waves, Jersey
on the dark horizon,
next to red lights
on the boombox pulsing her song.

Forever now she flirts a light
from the boombox man.
He misses her cue. She gives
the camera an exasperated stare
before he lights, and she drags deep.

HEART-SHAPED RING

I want you more than a quarter.
You make me spin
chrome wheels and gears.
I could own this grocery store
but die without you,
shiny purple anodized
baby in a plastic bubble
that opens with a pop.
Your unpolished seam
scrapes my finger lovingly.
Do you know how far you'll travel,
from house to house,
lost between cushions,
found in nightstands?
Rolling in my palm,
you circle the world.
You hardly weigh a thing.

SAINT JOHN

On a dark night, happy, burning
with want, I went unnoticed
from my quiet house in shadow,
took the back stairs without stopping.
Disguised, that moonless night,
in secret and without light,
no guide but my desire, I walked
as sure as noon to where he waited
to know me well, where no one saw.

Night that guided me, I thank you.
Night that united lover and beloved,
beloved and Love, night more lovable
than dawn, you taught my heart to grow flowers
for him alone as he lay sleeping
and I touched his hair beneath the fanning cedar.
He reached so calmly for my neck and wounded
   me there,
I hardly felt myself stop breathing,
but I stayed, and I forgot myself.
I rested my face on him and let everything go,
every worry to the grass, all harm forgotten.

THE MEMORY ROAD

What we did before talking in my car
the night lightning kept plucking the road ahead
out from darkness has gone to darkness,

but the fingermarks on your neck I still see.
You said a guy choked you. And you passed out.
I must have asked you to say more, just not

well enough. The scar of my silence keeps
growing like the abortion did in you
that summer you fought against me holding

your wrists to stop you from hitting your head
to knock the memories out and me saying,
"No, not if I'm around." I wouldn't be.

ELEGY FOR MR. OUTERSPACE

In the RV to Salvation Mountain,
the radio preacher
brayed of the abomination of desolation

you were passed out on the bed
head doing the junkie roll
at every dip

over the dry stream beds
with signs that said
Caution, Wrath of God Ahead.

You woke up for the mountain,
and getting drunk on the Slabs,
you Cupid lipped, lean cheeked, curly haired

boy who forged Lady Diana's signature
on that book of Keats you stole from me
to sell on eBay. So much broken at Forest Lawn:

the one I loved who used to call you her son
cried to see you; your parents
taking turns beside you—

not speaking. You silent.
Would you have smiled
to see yourself in all that makeup and satin?

Mr. Outerspace is dead,
gone to his death's bed,
under the recessed lighting.

ELEGY FOR HUNT

At Philippe's sandwiches,
clowns and mayors share the wall
with Hunt—
porn stache, red polyester vest,
ruffled shirt, and leer—
his finger sticking out
for one of the parrots he kept
in his East Hollywood one-bedroom

Hunt he did, always, not just in bars
but in amusement parks
where his birds rode tricycles—

even that Orange County Christian
family man fell prey

That's what Hunt's tongue could do

One night, three women, six men—
the numbers mattered
the blood test came back
100 grand in debt

He didn't lose his leer
until he had to let the birds scatter
to friends and shelters

At County USC
the bug was eating his brain
he took half a minute to say
You . . . win . . . dow un . . . der . . . sss . . . here . . .
eyes rolling around the room

He'd said *window*
which was like glass
so I gave him the plastic cup
of taxpayer ice water

and left to try to see him
parrots singing and dancing
his stache and leer

CUPID'S GALAXIES

Call it a starburst
Call it a bulge

a steady ratio of light
to spinning emptiness

Call it the dark percent
everything's curving into

but for the stars and us—eyes alight
in violent ballet

burning as we fall
from darkness into darkness

OFFICE BACCHUS

Tuesday at 10, he drops in, immortal
son of the CEO, his wrinkled, wine-
stained trench coat sweeping the cleanup schedule
off the break room fridge as he leaves the shrine
of donut box and coffee pot empty.
Once in his swivel chair slouched, he regales
beige acolytes with the follies Chablis
fueled that weekend in Vegas, with e-mails
that flow from static-shooting fingertips.
Out his story ripples; spreadsheets billow
like canvas; the boat of enterprise slips
into daydreams where grinning dolphins blow
hot fermented snot on PowerPoint slides,
and bosses throw themselves upon the tides.

OFFICE VENUS

Three cigarette butts,
all with the same pink lipstick,
bent on the sidewalk

near the thick ficus
in the manicured garden
beside Building O.

Yesterday, April,
the temp down in Fulfillment,
leaned warm denim here.

I can imagine
her curved fingernails flicking
still-smoking butts down,

then rubbing them out
with the ball of one of those
arched and sandaled feet,

calling the sitter
about her toddler, the world's
most lovable boy,

then turning angry,
blowing thick shafts of hot smoke
out her nose when she

hears Thing Like a Man
is late with the child support,
so mad that she makes

a nearby sparrow
stop poking for grubs among
the blue-veined violets

that sport bright snail trails
to look up at her, and while
a handful of bees

ply their honest trade
pushing the sugar, she makes
her bracelets ring when

with another drag
she laments, "I don't know what
I'm going to do,"

she can't ask her mom,
still disappointed in her,
who said, "What you need

are some decent clothes."
Forget it. "Maybe Aidon?"
she goes all mock-tragic—

"You know he murdered
this poor heart of mine! Besides,
he never returns my calls."

And certainly not
that workaholic welder
she's still technically

married to—"What do
I say? I'm really sorry
I wrecked your truck,

I guess I was drunk?"
She'd laugh if she did not fear
she will lose her home

if Thing, the lean teen
bike messenger, can't get
his mom to help out,

so she looks around,
sees the sparrow up on toes
to take six quick licks

from the dribbling head
of a sprinkler, when a gust
of wind pulls at her

silk scarf, and inspires
the sparrow, almost too fat
to fly, into air,

wings a feathery
thwbt and suddenly wanting
to graze her shoulder

and nibble her ear,
yesterday, when April was
burning her Kools here.

But she's not here now.
She got let go yesterday—
left us to winter.

THE LAW OFFICE FATES

Even the managing partner is nice
to those three old women in the basement
with linoleum and fluorescent lights,
though above ground he makes sure the firm's all
white carpet and shine. Toner fingerprints
smudge the tape that holds the *You Want It When?*
cartoon's hysteria to the yellowed wall.

Layoffs pass them over, perhaps because
their postal scales know the price, and their Bates
stamps count each page, of every petition
that by bike messenger flies to the judge.
Prayers for relief they answer, however,
in order received, and sometimes kindly.
Their sewing kit has stitched many summers'
bargain coats into courtroom readiness.

Some argue they blindly obey the boss;
others, that their shiny Selectric sphere,
in striking digit to paper, calls forth
the real fiscal year. All remember
the client who called them "those weird old hags"
died before he could win his appeal.

OFFICE CUPID

Chubby and short, with Coke-bottle glasses
in wrinkled Dockers and puffy white shirt
he brings heartache to the cubicled masses,
the pimp supreme of their sugar and dirt.
Thanks to him, Celestina from HR's
kid won the high school contest for selling
a hundred boxes of stale chocolate bars.
Everyone knows, but nobody's telling
how he humbled that horndog harasser,
the big exec, by pushing his mail cart
across department lines, and with a whisper
in Sales and his back to the board, tossed dart,
hit red. He'll be fired for contempt of cash
but'll do swell. His market doesn't crash.

OFFICE APOLLO

Friday's fiery orange octopus sunset
wreathes his brow as he drives his elliptical
in his corner suite. A dead string quartet
purrs from speakers. "It's only cyclical,"
he soothes his team via Delphos headset,
"The numbers will balance by end of day
in London. We can always float the debt."
On his desk, the contract lies in disarray.
Heroic labors yet remain. Good thing
he already bought that hyacinth bouquet—
a hundred pages will need perfecting
before his diva daughter ends her ballet.
For now, each clause will meet his crow-sharp eye.
The new paralegal, Daphne, walks by.

TO THE SUN

All life's maker and destroyer-to-be,
this flesh, this fire and fuel recite the mass
of conversion of dark to what can see
the hot bead of a magnifying glass
pull smoke from yellow leaves. The scent's yours too.
Carbon's forge is no cottage deity
but a steel mill in elemental stew,
diamonds boiling in a spherical sea.
But even you will suffer entropy.
You'll swell up like a corpse and disappear
into the clock's gears. We'll be Semele.
No rainbow or fire will always live here.
But another evening is coming soon.
Time to make soup, puff on the glowing spoon.

CLOCK

After I fell asleep, trees sprung and flared and fell.
My hands trembled as I dreamed that an empire stormed
across the mantelpiece, and silence overcame
the school. The Milky Way unwound. Insurance men
in raincoats poured out across the city, with plans
spiral bound in black briefcases, until downtown
marched behind cranes to the bending river. Grown old,
grandkids sat on porches and took up the lap steel
guitar or shuffled twelve old pinup girls, seconds
of pie waiting on plates, while watching grandchildren
at play outside, their faces blurring over mine,
one spring afternoon that seemed to last forever.

BUYING A BLAKE CALENDAR

I buy it for another year—
a folded paper raft of hope
to ride to freedom on Friday
and dances in the local square—
with bills I tender to the river
of the till to show I am not lost.

But I must already be lost
if a press release about my year
is what I bottle for the river
of time, telling how I caught hope's
brass rings by toeing to the square-
edged prophecy of each Friday.

So on end of business Friday
I'll be as godless and as lost
as now, one uncovenanted square
slouching out the Möbius year
with what seven gods give of hope
to one sinking in the river.

But then nothing keeps the river
from growing new trees on Friday
to show I cannot erase hope
or keep a day from getting lost
among the folds of the paper year
that never fits inside its square.

The Ancient of Days holds the square
of gold rays that free the river
to run its living course and year
and promise me every Friday
since the gnomon never gets lost
walking its figure-eights of hope.

Fifty-two rows may channel hope
and pencils circle each square
in acts of counting what is lost
and found flowing in the river
to be forgotten by Friday
and give to life another year.

Papers get lost, but the river
floods the local square on Friday
with mud and hope for another year.

OUR STORY SO FAR

I run, I climb, I scratch my head
always imagining downstream
some green wake of me trails off into you.
Truth is, you flow through me.
In the unfrayable ripple of your hem
all the spider stars spin.

NO

There is no such thing as society. There are individual men and women, and there are families. "There is" is a weak construction. There's no reason to use "there is." There is no soup. There is no "there is." There is only "there is," because there is no alternative. If there's nothing there, there's no "there" there. The notes, the text, all say no. Sisyphus walks along the shore, skipping stones of negation. Because there ain't no   way   other way   reason   sense in trying   doubt   fooling   use excuse   denying   tomorrow   way you can tell   way it's true   way it ain't   grace period   dope   hope   getting there from here

OFFICE CASSANDRA

Among the interns, flacks,
account execs, stooges, sharks,
rookies, schnooks, temps, idiot
sons-in-law, geeks, big shots,
lackeys, snakes, suckups, peons,
and the dork with the company blog,
she types another memo.

OFFICE 9/11

I'd run the phone line out next to my bed on the porch because I was renting out the bedroom, so when the call woke me up, I said hello without opening my eyes. It was my boss. I thought I was really late, but it wasn't that, he said look at the television, and he told me I didn't have to come in because maybe there would be trouble at the World Trade Center in L.A. because he had anxiety. Our offices were across the street. But I didn't argue about a day off, and I went to the living room and turned on the TV and watched the planes fly into the towers over and over, and the TV kept talking with aggressive innocence about how unbelievable it was, but it wasn't, and I started waiting for the names to learn like Breitweiser, O'Neill, Rescorla, and Briley, who was maybe that man in the picture who, like the others at the office that day, having to choose between fire and falling, stepped into the sky.

OFFICE MARS

Phalanxed in brass, he enters central command
and pulls a laptop from a general's hand;
his grimace accelerates and head tilts back
to trifocal a night vision attack
of green insurgent dots upon a convoy.
From satellites his orders boom: destroy
the spires from which the enemy's firing.
Soon bombs bloom yellow, and dust and smoke ring
the dark machines escaping. "I can't see,"
he jokes to General Jumper, "just what we
pay you for. Is it time for your pension?"
Thus roused, he gives the budget attention.
With each new war, his faith in spreadsheets grows,
with dollars in columns and blood in the rows.

SAMUEL TELLS SAUL

Ban the medium. Shoot the message.
Make your children stop singing.

Tell the metal rain to fall
until Venus swallows her final pills.

Explain that the war brought you here—
they'll say they understand

everywhere miracles are spreading.
So go out tonight in disguise,

see the witch because
you aren't getting any answers

from prophets, stones, or dreams.
She may be surprised as you

to see me rising from the ground
to say, god would never forgive what you do,

and for adding to the infinite sorrows of Mary Lincoln,
tomorrow you and your sons will be with me.

WARPLANE TAROT

P-38: Burbank's five-sworded,
counter-rotating, fork-tailed
child of Operation Vengeance,
in thousands
you strafed the nightmares
of the survivors of your whisper
as Californian as surf guitar.

B-58: you were the master
of time to climb to alabaster
atmosphere, four engines roaring
to silent desert parking lot, you cost
10 cups of gold. Nuclear club,
you almost waged the micrometer's war
against the flesh falling from a tower.

F-35: you're the zero at the game's end,
grounded angel that may be
the chariot that kills every enemy
for all our money, dancing
in a dumb show that ends
when you strangle your pilot,
you crown our supersonic frailty.

HORAPOLLO'S HIEROGLYPHICS

When they draw a man with a rifle
they show the destruction of a city.

To show the destruction of a nation,
they draw a hooded man holding out his arms.

When they draw a burning book,
they mean a scholar tortured until conversion.

What of a crazy lady feeding pigeons?
The defeated hunger for redemption.

By the disc of the sun they mean
the wheel that can't be seen turning.

By sacred words written in a spiral?
A calligrapher shot dead in the street.

What do they mean by crickets?
They mean the disappeared.

What do they mean by a wasp?
War's jaw, wings, and sting.

What do they mean by a star?
The god of darkness, staring into fire.

By one who shouts from a tower they mean
one made to watch his wife

and family killed one by one.
They hang his portrait in the classroom

where by *x* they mean *y*.
The heart is too empty or too full,

so how do they show the scales that will not settle?
By Libra, dangling as it flies.

TO MONEY

In the rainbow-ceilinged hotel foyer
motivational syllables sail
out from the follow-your-bliss seminar.
The Goldberg Variations rain upon
a figure-eighting fly. Conversations
buzz around you, arpeggios that start
"I love . . . ." Outside, a girl with a tattoo
that rounds her shoulder slowly works a broom
kitchenward, the hand-blown window panes
bending her in silence from youth to age.

THE VOICES

THE NAMES

for all the innocent people who surely lived in Amiriyah
say

Jake W. Suter Khalil al-Zahawi
say

Noor Elhuda Saad Hamoodi baby Basra
Dr. Ihab Abed 34 Basra

Wife of Rebee Abdullah adult female Karma
names of the companies that have made money

Halliburton / KBR, TITAN, CACI, and Blackwater
never let the weight of this combination endanger

I have never been so blessed as the day I met
Melissa Dawn Benfield.

Please keep our babies safe.
Love Always, Your husband, Jess.

Matthew R. Hennigan Previous 100 | Next 100
I fled today out of the army.

What is there done, my son?
Kenneth Michael Kays November 29, 1991

THE PLEA

How long, Sovereign Lord, holy and true,
How long shall we lay dead in the street of the great city?

My uncle was in Vietnam, he didn't make it too good
cause he came back homeless himself

twenty-two suicides a day—
those who speak, pay.

Let now the astrologers
the monthly prognosticators stand up and save you

the next six months are crucial
You want 1950? We can do 1950. You want 1389?

The prayer for relief demands judgment
will any jury convict on this evidence?

Of wars worse than civil   and crime set loose
we sing   how Rome's high race

her victorious sword   plunged in her vitals
armies of kin embattled.   put your bodies

upon the gears and upon the wheels, upon the levers,
you've got to indicate to the people who run it

Why should we hear about body bags and deaths?
So why should I waste my beautiful mind on something
like that?

80,000 tons
300 civilian deaths per thousand tons

Did he say anything, Colonel Sullivan later asked,
about the five children . . . being killed on the bed?

U.S. District Judge T.S. Ellis III overturned the jury award
I will not take that which is thine for the Lord

THE POETS

And as to the poets, those who go astray follow them
Their banquets are accompanied

by tambourine and flute, and by wine
amidst gardens and fountains

cornfields and palm-trees laden with fruit
dwellings in the mountains and leading a wanton life

Are you ashamed of love? Ashamed of me?
I no longer have the slightest concern

for arms and the man, I want a woman's arms!
The poets must give us imagination of peace

They look behind at every step & believe it is a dream,
singing empire is no more

Caesar's might is in armies
in love conquered nations count for nothing

He that ruled nations in anger is persecuted
They break into song:

Are you weak like us now?
Are you like us now?

THE LIARS

Where have you made a raid today?
And David said, *against the Negev of Judah.*

Travel in the land and see
what was the end of those who rejected truth

You surely will not die! Your eyes will be opened
Every effort was made to spare innocent life

massive amounts of food   the price is worth it
money that would be used for their well-being

One was a con artist, code-named "Curveball"
The other reportedly sent to Egypt and tortured

We will not rest until we find him
three shots to the forehead

This confrontation is willed by God, who wants
to use this conflict to erase his people's enemies

And none but the guilty led us astray
suggesting policy naming language proposing strategy

around Tikrit and Baghdad and east, west, south,
and north, we create our own reality

You sold yourself for nothing.
You shall be redeemed without money.

THE PICTURES

We're functioning in a—with peacetime restraints, with legal requirements in a wartime situation, in the information age, where people are running around with digital cameras and taking these unbelievable photographs and then passing them off, against the law, to the media, to our surprise, when they had not even arrived in the Pentagon.

I saw the translator Abu Hamid fucking a kid, Hilas stated. The kid was hurting very bad and they covered all the doors with sheets. Then when I heard screaming I climbed the door because on top it wasn't covered and I saw Abu Hamid, who was wearing the military uniform, putting his dick in the little kid's ass. And the female soldier was taking pictures.

THE SNIPER

They made no move during the night, saying,
At dawn we'll kill him.

His breathing, his pulse, his delivery, his eyes, his lead
Why, they couldn't hit an elephant at this dist . . .

The judgments of the Lord are true and righteous
A little bit larger than your thumb

Whoever falls on this stone shall be broken
All who use swords will be killed with swords

Ten empires fell on this grease spot
Very difficult to hit a running man at 400, 500 yards

The slow ones are all gone
Your heart shall meditate terror. Time of flight:

three seconds. 22,000 square miles of territory.
Just enough to bury our dead.

Along the trench, sometimes a bullet sang.
Death, many deaths I'll sing.

THE WARNING

Woe unto them that are wise in their own eyes
Death will find you, even if you are in towers

and burning instead of beauty
and houses without men

I have given you warning in fairness
I am bringing a distant nation against you

No man shall spare his brother
Deserted she will lie upon the ground

in front of the grave of her love
talking to the stone   in broken sentences

The crimes of this guilty land
will never be purged away but with blood

Well, since we took a life, our life is next
That's how everybody was living

$12 billion in shrink-wrapped $100 bills
363 tons loaded onto C-130 cargo planes

offered to idols from blood, from things strangled
from those who blow on knots

sow the wind
where rust and moth destroyeth

every nation shall be called to its book
The Lord visits the iniquity of the fathers

on the children and the children's children

ACKNOWLEDGMENTS

JOURNALS

"Aerospace Tarot" appeared in *Drunk Monkeys* magazine and *Levure littéraire 10: Words and Declarations of War: The Unannounced Death of Language*.

"Astro Cupid" and "A Fool's Journey" appeared in *Mouse Tales*.

"Hieroglyphics" appeared in *Hartskill Review* and *Levure littéraire 10: Words and Declarations of War: The Unannounced Death of Language*.

"Office Bacchus" appeared in *Blinders Literary Journal*.

"Redhead Venus" and "Heart-Shaped Ring" appeared in *Cultural Weekly*.

"To the Terrace House" appeared in *Crony* magazine.

"To PTSD" appeared in *Black Heart Magazine*.

"Traveling Man" appeared in *The Gambler Mag*.

"The Unicorn" appeared in *Glitterwolf*.

"Walking along Sunset Weighing Pieces of Plastic with My Drug Dealer's Pocket Scale" appeared in *Askew*.

"Astro Cupid," "Clock," and "Our Story So Far" appeared in *Syzygy Poetry Journal*.

ANTHOLOGIES

"To Sacks, a Costumer" appeared in *Eating Her Wedding Dress: A Collection of Clothing Poems* (Ragged Sky Press).

"To the Terrace House" appeared in *Wide Awake: Poets of Los Angeles and Beyond* (Pacific Coast Poetry Series).

"The Voices" appeared in the anthology *Revolutionary Poets Brigade* (Vagabond).

"The Voices" is an editorial poem constructed of quotes from various sources under the doctrine of fair use. While diligent effort was made to obtain permission from each copyright holder, we regret any omissions in including permissions at the time of this printing.

NOTES

“Blind Date” is a landay.

“How a Flower Became a Stone” is a translation of a selection of Ovid’s *Metamorphoses.*

“Riding to the L.A. River Bike Path” is a translation of a poem of Horace.

“Saint John” is a translation of a poem by the Spanish mystic Saint John of the Cross.

Speakers in “The Voices” include the angel Gabriel, Jesus, David, Jeremiah, Abraham Lincoln, Dwight Eisenhower, Satan, Madeleine Albright, Donald Rumsfeld, George Bush, Barbara Bush, a television pundit, Ovid, Propertius, William Blake, Walt Whitman, Allen Ginsberg, Mario Savio, a homeless veteran, a former prisoner, and John Brown.

Eric Howard studied poetry with Robert Mezey and Karen Swenson at the Claremont Colleges before working as a substitute junior high school, high school, and college teacher while living in the Los Angeles neighborhood of Silver Lake. He later obtained a master's degree in English from California State University while studying prosody with Henri Coulette. He currently lives near the Los Angeles River and its bike path.